Venomous Relationships

Veteran Baltimore 911 Operator exposes common toxic relationships

Certified Life Coach Tamara Neal

Copyright © 2014 Tamara Neal
All rights reserved.
No part of this book may be used or reproduced in any manner whatsoever
without the written
permission of the Publisher.

ISBN: 0990937909
ISBN 13: 9780990937906
Library of Congress Control Number: 2014918672
Tamara's Book Publishing Service
Gwynn Oak, Maryland

This book is dedicated with Love
To the person that is
Sick and tired
Of being
Sick and tired
Of Venomous Relationships
Although, I do not wish to impose my religious beliefs on you, I pray that
after reading this book
You will be able to acknowledge,
What you perhaps, already know,
And ultimately, make a decision to love yourself enough, to only desire,
A healthy, stable relationship,
That will be the epitome of love
1 Corinthians 13:4-8 (New International Version)
4 Love is patient, love is kind. It does not envy, it does not boast, it is not
proud. 5 It is not rude, it is not self-seeking, it is not easily angered, it keeps
no record of wrongs. 6 Love does not delight in evil but rejoices with the
truth.

7 It always protects, always trusts, always hopes, always perseveres. . 8 Love
never fails. But where there are prophecies, they will cease; where there are
tongues, they will be stilled; where there is knowledge, it will pass away.

Acknowledgements

~

I thank and acknowledge the following people, for the many acts of love, support, encouragement and kindness,
During the labor and birthing process of my new book
Venomous Relationships!
To my husband Freddie,
For joining me on this journey, believing in me, providing an unconditional arsenal of encouragement, support, inspiration and
Love,
To my sons; Corey, Fred, Anthony and Brandon,
For providing pertinent information, continuous love and support,
My daughter Danielle,
Daughter in-law Demetrius and Future daughter in-law Candice,
For their loving input, support and continuous encouragement,
My grandchildren,
For their enthusiasm, countless hugs, kisses, laughs and Unconditional love

My Dad Donald and Mom, the late Brenda Taylor
For
A lifetime of love and encouragement
Teaching me how to walk the road less traveled, and finally,
 How to fly!

Contents

Introduction

I wrote Venomous Relationships to prevent other women from facing the common, silent relationship heartbreak that I have not only seen happen too many of my friends, family, and acquaintances but have also experienced myself. It is often very difficult for a woman to admit that she is indeed being emotionally abused, particularly if she is competent and successful in other areas of her life. I needed to find a way to get the attention of women suffering from the silent trauma of emotional abuse (whether or not they also experience physical abuse).

I believe that although the number of women that suffer from recognized abuse is overwhelming, far too many cases go unrecognized because when a woman suffers from emotional abuse, the emotionally abusive husband or lover uses a variety of tactics that damage her self-esteem, and she excuses inexcusable behavior. At that point, she wants to give her partner the benefit of the doubt rather than throw him out or expose him. This is especially true when the person is a good provider or has been good to her in other ways. We learn how to rationalize what has been totally irrational, and we become quite good at it.

The abuser's goal is to make his partner believe that she is stupid, ugly, and unlovable—at the minimum. He will often inform his victim that she is lucky to have him, is not as good-looking as the other women in his past, doesn't satisfy him in the bedroom, and that his family doesn't think she is good enough for him.

I wrote Venomous Relationships with love, to expose the most common, silently abusive relationships and to teach women how to avoid them. (In some, women have unknowingly been colluding in the abuse themselves.) I call out obvious red-flag behaviors such as addiction, physical abuse, and adultery, but I also highlight lesser-known signs of relationship trouble, including indications that a potential partner is only interested in a one-night stand or that a partner hasn't gotten over his previous relationship and is thus in no position to make the new one work. Throughout the book, I remind the reader that there's only one person she can and should change: herself. The energy a woman spends chasing one of these bad-news partners could be better spent learning to improve and care for herself, building the internal strength needed to avoid any partner who doesn't trust or care for her.

Venomous Relationships takes a direct approach. It skips the jargon and reads like a girlfriend chat in a coffee shop. Each chapter includes a Scenario of a venomous relationship filled will all of the trauma and drama, some parts of which are hard to swallow—but a reality check always is. Then there's the Let's Talk section, which is like a coffee-shop chat about the scenario. Many women who suffer from abuse don't have girlfriends because they have been isolated from the world by design. It's OK; you have a girlfriend now.

I skip the jargon and the traditional language of psychology here; I prefer a personal approach, encouraging the reader to just recognize and reclaim a lot of what she might already know: to heal, we must feel. Readers can only find the self-confidence they seek within themselves.

The Conclusion section is a review of the venomous relationship from the chapter, identifying its telltale traits and discussing the red flags in the abusive person that his partner missed when she first met him, and how to release anger and heal the damage so that she can avoid repeating the pattern. Finally, a Today I will Release and Let Go of page has been provided at the end of each chapter. This page is for the reader to document some of what they may already know but have refused to acknowledge.

OK, let's get started! I hope that at the end of each chapter, you feel inspired enough to move on to the next. I desire to introduce the reader to someone who has been seeking to be loved unconditionally for many years through various relationships. She is cracked but not broken, and certainly worthy of repair.

You will need a mirror and time to learn to love the person in the mirror. You'll need an open mind and a strong desire to acknowledge the role that you've played in toxic relationships. You'll need time to heal and time to learn how to love someone else to receive the full benefit from this book!

1

Dr. Respectable and Mr. Hide

~

One bright, sunny day, you and your two precious daughters are standing in the roller coaster line at the local amusement park. Virtually appearing out of nowhere behind you is a gentleman with a very familiar face, though you can't place him. Looking delighted to see you, he says hi and calls you by your first and last name. Needless to say, you are too embarrassed to let the gentleman know that you don't remember him, so you pretend you do. When you step up to get on the roller coaster, he says in a cheerful voice, "I got my partner," and places his arm around your shoulder, escorting you to the next available car behind your daughters. This is really convenient for you, because you really were not interested in riding alone.

As the ride leaves the ground, you realize that perhaps letting your children talk you into getting on wasn't such a good idea. Suddenly, you are overwhelmed with fear, and the courage that you had on the ground is overridden by the terror you experience 160 feet in the air. As you scream, beg, and plead for mercy, the man never takes his eyes off you and laughs. When the ride returns to the dock, almost like a different person, he's full of compassion and says, "Let's go get some ice cream." Instantly your gut tells you that this will not be your last roller coaster ride with this guy.

Eventually, you discover that he is the gentleman that used to wave to you in the morning when you walked your daughters to school. He is fairly attractive and quickly lets you know that he has been checking you out for quite some time from a distance. You are flattered and shocked, since you hadn't noticed him at all and were apparently not interested. Now that he has made his presence known, it seems almost impossible to go anywhere in the neighborhood without seeing him by some strange coincidence. You are at a yard sale, and he just happens to drive by. You are walking your dog, and there he is, walking his. When you arrive home at night, he just happens to be sitting on his front porch.

One day, after several declined invitations, you accept a date to the movies. During the discovery period of the date, you learn that he is very single, have never married, have no children, has a fairly decent job, and is not afraid of commitment. He also reveals that he has observed the fact that your daughters have different fathers and that you apparently make poor choices in men. He expresses a desire to show you what a real man is, if given the opportunity.

From that day forward, he starts showing up at your job with flowers, and your coworkers are all impressed. He refuses to allow you to wash your car or do anything that he considers not ladylike. You have truly struck gold with this guy!

Although you just met a few months ago, he has managed to convince you that the two of you are inseparable and that you are the woman of his dreams. He has moved into your apartment. It makes sense to save the money, because he is always there anyway. It feels good to have someone that is willing to spend good quality time with you, and he is very persuasive, at getting you to accept his point of view, regardless of how you may feel about the matter at hand.

Your friends think that he is a bit weird and tell you to be careful, but you think that they are just jealous because he requires so much of your time. Besides, he doesn't think that much of them either and has hinted to you that your so-called friends appear to be a bit envious and would switch places with you in a heartbeat, if he would have them. Eventually, he manages to find fault in all of your friends and most of your family members. Whenever the telephone rings, he becomes instantly annoyed. He has made it clear to you, unlike the previous men that you had in your life, he is a dedicated family man and therefore he thinks your time at home should be spent with him exclusively, without any interruption, from an outside source, period.

One day, your car, which had always been faithful, apparently just dies. He gladly steps in and is willing to drive you around from point A to point B. From that day forward, the two of you are like twins. Ultimately, he persuades you to marry him and move to a secluded area, with hopes of living happily, ever after.

Six months later, the honeymoon is over. You no longer have a car for him to wash, and flowers only get delivered at work after bad arguments. Now he is constantly putting you down, occasionally pushing you, complaining about your weight, and correcting you. One day your cup runs over. You look at him and yell, "Get out!" When you wake up, he's putting ice on your lip and begging you to never make him smack you again! When the kids come home, you immediately start protecting your abuser by lying to the kids about what happened to you. He takes them out so you can get some rest, you start blaming yourself for him smacking you, and he returns with flowers.

For a while, things are great, and he keeps his promise by never smacking you again. One day, you turn your back on him while he's talking, and he shoves you down twelve steps headfirst. Instead of calling an ambulance, he nurses you back to health himself. Now, unable to work, you are completely dependent on him financially for everything, and because of the abuse, mentally you start to feel like you need him.

You find yourself afraid to let people know that you are in a hopeless, helpless situation once again. Sadly, you withdraw from your family and friends. You have chosen isolation over public disgrace and embarrassment. You only have two close friends now. One of them is Disgrace, and the other is Shame.

Your soul cries out to be restored, but it falls on deaf ears. You are in a total state of denial and have lost your ability to listen to your own internal instincts. You have been accused of being sneaky and unfaithful so often that you are beginning to wonder if there could possibly be any truth to it. He constantly blames you and others for all of his shortcomings, character defects, and problems. His drinking is definitely out of control, and he has no problem destroying your property and anything that you value when he is in a rage. If you manage to stay out of the range of fire until he passes out or gets tired, you've just had a good day.

After three black eyes, countless bloody noses, two missing teeth, four broken fingers, two hospitalizations, and several domestic violence court appearances with charges you can no longer drop, he decides you will never get the opportunity to send him to jail again! It has now become crystal clear to you: the next time he sends you flowers after a beating, you will not be at work! Finally, the fear of staying has outweighed the terror of leaving, and you have decided to be a survivor instead of a statistic.

Let's Talk

It is very difficult to determine what type of person you may be dating in the beginning, because both people have their best foot forward. It is our human nature to make an impact on people with all of our good qualities early on in a relationship. Every person has an alter ego that they introduce to people when they first meet. What you want to look for are signs of the person being their authentic-self. Real men are self-confident, and secure, not cocky and conceited. The difference is easy to identify over time. Conceited people can be defensive, competitive, arrogant, and sometimes hostile. When a person is truly self-confident they have a sense of inner security, assurance and composure. When a man is unsure of himself – he will often talk too much or too little, too fast or too slow. Proceed with caution if he sees no need for you to be involved in the conversation, or he expects you to carry the entire conversation. Authentic people are usually not overly sensitive, easily threatened, hurt, or determined to win you over to their point of view. When a man is sure of himself he is okay with you having your own opinion, realizes that you are entitled to it and will not feel a pressing need to convince you that he is right all the time. A man with a well-developed self-concept will know how to manage anger in a positive way. Anyone can be provoked to anger but it should not be explosive and damaging to others.

Character defects cannot truly be hidden, regardless of how manipulative the person may be. Often, the way a person treats other people will give you a pretty good idea of what type of person you will be dealing with later. Does he often suffer from road rage? How he treats his mother is almost a foolproof sign of how he will treat you later on down the road. What type of father is he? When he is angry, does he use abusive language and throw things?

Many women see these kinds of behavior in the very beginning but refuse to acknowledge the flares going off because they want so desperately for this person to be different from their past failures. People can be really deceptive should always be regarded with some suspicion when you first meet. The only thing that you should assume about any strange person is that you won't assume anything. If he seems too good to be true, then he probably is.

Conclusion

Being subjected to abuse is a humiliating and demeaning experience and will most often leave you feeling very ashamed. Although, this may offer very little comfort, it is important for you at this critical time to understand that other people's opinion of you is not your reality and therefore none of your business. You are not alone; your problem is very common. On average, 24 people per minute are victims of rape, physical violence or stalking by an intimate partner in the United States — more than 12 million women and men over the course of a year.[According to statistics, provided by the National Domestic Violence Hotline}

No man is perfect, so if you think that you have found a man that is, stay tuned. More will be revealed. Learn to trust your intuition, and never ignore something that troubles you so much that you feel it in your gut. When you have a gut feeling, it is your body's natural way of telling you something. It could be that something is not right about the situation. Take time to get to know a person in every season before you conclude that he is God's gift to women. This guy made you feel uncomfortable right from the start, but you refused to acknowledge the flares going off, because you wanted so badly for him to really be your knight in shining armor.

It is not uncommon for an abuser to act like the guy of any woman's dreams, especially after a violent episode. This is known as the vicious cycle, and it will continue as long as you allow him in your life without treatment from an outside source. Once he feels that he has gained your trust again, he is intentionally cruel to you, belligerent, combative, and militant. His goal is to make you think that he is all you need and that the two of you only have each other. To isolate you from family and friends is his ultimate goal so that he can—privately, quietly, and without interruption—slip you into his torture chamber.

He may even try to make you feel guilty by threatening to commit suicide if you leave him. Leave, and don't look back. Take whatever steps that is necessary for you to recreate your life without him intimately involved in it and learn how to survive in your new environment, gradually.

Although, hurting people, hurt people, be mindful that you will never be able to hurt your abuser, by HATING him. You will only continue to allow the abuser to live in your head, long after the relationship is over and ultimately hurt yourself. Although, you may not feel like forgiving your abuser at this time, make a decision to forgive him as soon as possible. Forgiveness is a decision not a feeling. Only after you are able to release and let go, of the pain, from the past, will you be able to see the true beauty of the present and reap the benefits of the future.

Today I will Release and Let Go of :

2

The Playa from the Himalaya

~

Your girlfriend begs you to go out to the club with her to celebrate your newfound freedom after a much-needed breakup. It actually took very little convincing. Although there was something inside you that said "Stay home," something outside of you asked, "What are you staying home for?"

It's a hot summer night, and you're looking even hotter wearing the little black dress that you bought after you realized that somehow, you shed twenty-five pounds effortlessly after going through your most recent stressful relationship when Jenny Craig, a protein diet, meal-replacement shakes, gym memberships, and countless diet pills failed miserably at getting rid of them.

So you go to the club with absolutely zero expectation of meeting anyone, planning perhaps to share a drink or two with your friends and perhaps some girl talk. Then he walks over and introduces himself. You end up having the good time that you had been waiting for your ex to show you for the last seven years of your life together, but he only recognized the world of sports. Maybe he'd look at you if you screamed "Look at me!"

This guy offers to buy you a drink and is very friendly. He knows just what to say and how to say it, and he's well built, too. Although you've met countless men of his demeanor, this time it's different. Gorgeous George has a magnetism about him that, after a few drinks, makes what first appeared a dim, dreary place into a romantic oasis. Shortly afterward, it seems that all of your dreams might be coming true.

Needless to say, like so many other women you know, you have had your fair share of one-night stands, booty calls, baby daddies and deadbeat dads. But although you know all the tricks, you still look for treats. So when the club closes, like Cinderella leaving the ball, you dismiss the girlfriend that you rode to the club with. Mesmerized by this guy's immaculate car (also known as "the chick magnet"), you proudly get in as if you just won a prize and proceed to give directions to your place—like a sheep following a shepherd to the slaughter!

Like numerous times before, your gut is talking, but your brain isn't listening. At some point, you even think that you can make this person fall in love with you by being seductively submissive. So you allow your panties to hit the floor before the first date is over.

Last night was great. This morning he appears to be in a hurry. So, like a doctor going to deliver a baby, this once-passionate gentleman rushes out of your life without a kiss good-bye or a glance back. Almost immediately, you feel played. But how can this be possible when you were such a willing participant?

So you spend the day on the telephone with your girlfriend that you dismissed, talking about the great time that you had last night. Finally, you decide to call him and notice that your call goes straight to a voice mail system that is not set up yet. Days go by without a phone call from him, and the telephone number that he gave you apparently isn't correct.

Concerned about his well-being and having no other contact information for him, you venture back to the killing grounds—the club where you met him—hoping to see him. And you do. There he is, looking just as charismatic as he did on the day you met, only he's not alone, and he treats you like a stalker invading his territory.

～〇

Let's Talk

Your stock fell when your panties hit the floor on the first date. Don't expect this guy to see you as someone he would take home to meet his mother. You set the stage, made him the superstar, and you played the role of an extra. The Playa from the Himalaya feels that you had your one minute of fame, and he has moved on to the next audition. There is only one person that this guy allows himself to have any genuine feeling for, and he visits that person regularly—when he looks in the mirror.

Some women have decided to accommodate Playas of this type by accepting the booty call position. This simply means that when a guy like this has a bad night at the club, he calls you at some ungodly hour, and you open the door when he gets there. If something in your gut tells you that you deserve to be treated better than that, it is because you do.

These Playas don't have to be complete losses if you take them for what they're worth—and that is a few free drinks and some dirty dancing. They are, for the most part, immature and unable to commit.

The Playa from the Himalaya is looking for someone to complete a fantasy and bores very easily. He is a hunter by nature. Although the Playa peruses a wide variety of prey, he is fairly selective about whom he chooses to play with. His goal is to hit a home run straight out of the club and into the unsuspecting prey's bedroom. Although he is not looking for a keeper, he considers his prey a trophy. Therefore, he often selects women who are superficial because they are more likely to believe that they are the best thing that ever happened to him and are usually starved for attention. So he makes them feel like they are the cream of the crop and waters them down real good. Yes, he has all eyes on you!

Boyfriend has no problem with leaving the club and going to your place for a sleepover. He will wait patiently for you to eat the bait that he has been feeding you and make you feel like you are the woman that he has been waiting for all his life. Once the heat is on, he will melt your heart and may even curl your toes. He is passionate and knows what to do and how to do it!

The next morning will be pretty much the same. Suddenly, he appears to be in a hurry and his conversation is now about his busy schedule and how he is going to try to get back to you tonight. Don't wait up, girlfriend. You have just been played, but don't get angry with him, because you were a willing participant. It is very important that you remember not to hate the Playa. Just stop playing the game.

Conclusion

Most Playas can be really deceptive and appear sincere. It's really hard to trust a guy with this mentality. He may even think he likes you and offer you a position as his doormat. This is a ground-level position that requires you to be walked on and to play detective with the many different women that are somehow constantly in your life.

Although your gut will tell you that you are being lied to and deserve more, your heart will tell you that it is all in the game of love. Remember, this man can be just like a drug. You will never get a high like the first again; you will only chase it. The only hope for a healthy, steady relationship with a Playa from the Himalaya is if he decides to put away his childish ways and become a man of integrity, but that is a process. Needless to say, there is nothing you can do to change him. He must make the decision himself.

Don't be a victim to someone who does not know who he is or what he wants. Find someone that is worth your time and your trust. If you truly enjoy being a social butterfly, fly away solo when the doors to the club close, and perhaps one day you will meet someone that is able to recognize your true beauty and will be worthy of your wings.

Tamara Neal

〜◯

Today I will Release and Let Go of:

3

Loving Mr. Video Madden

~

In the beginning, he made you feel young and vibrant. His spontaneity and childlike courtship style was very inviting and seemed to bring excitement to what was becoming a dull existence. He was a bit down on his luck and had just suffered the loss of another dead-end job because he claimed he didn't have proper transportation to get there.

You grew up with him, so he was no stranger to you, and once you discovered that he got along great with your kids, it was like a flashing neon green light saying to go full speed ahead with a relationship. You spent countless hours with him and your children playing video *Madden NFL*, and you thought at first that perhaps, life was taking a turn for the better. Although he was known as a bit of a bad boy, there was something alluring about him, and you feel like you want to give him a chance, because apparently, nobody else ever has.

You feel like this man loves you (although he has never really verbalized that), so you are willing to put up with his short-term employment and weekend parties. While you are at work, he plays video games and makes friends around the neighborhood. The girl next door is quite fond of him, and so is the babysitter.

His mother is so happy that the two of you are together, because he is no longer in her basement.

When he is sporting around in your car, the tank is always empty, and he gets lost on the way home. The pizza-delivery person puts his order in on Friday when he comes to work and is sitting in your living room playing the game and drinking beer with your guy when he gets off. Your man loves your cooking so much that he never takes you out to eat or cooks himself. A fifteen-year-old could only dream of having his tennis shoe collection. On weekends, it is mandatory that he goes out with his boys, and he is often caught holding female telephone numbers—for his friends, if you believe that.

Finally, after years without working, he gets a job. This is a welcome relief, because you are beginning to feel like you have adopted a teenage son instead of having a mate. Although the job doesn't pay much, you would have been happy with anything—however; his first paycheck is used to celebrate the new job. The second paycheck is used to purchase things that he couldn't buy when he was unemployed. By the third paycheck, he's beginning to get a little angry with you because he really doesn't appreciate you wanting to take all of his money when you're well aware that he really doesn't make that much.

By the end of the month, he's terminated for failing to report to work because although you woke him up before you left for your job, you didn't make sure that he was completely awake and he fell back to sleep. Needless to say, this was entirely your fault.

୧ଠ

Let's Talk

Boys are generally OK with lying around the house, eating, sleeping, and playing countless video games, while their mothers are working. *Men* support themselves (or don't seek a relationship until they are self-supporting). This guy is a "bad boy" because of the way that he treats women, and he has lots of problems. The fact that he often throws tantrums when he is confronted about his mischief and will rarely, if ever, admit to wrongdoing is testament to his immaturity and inability to commit.

Keep in mind that you can't teach old dogs new tricks. If this guy hasn't learned not to bite the hand that feeds him and never do his business in his own backyard by forty, he never will. Take him to the local pound and leave him. Let some lonely old lady give him a home. Now, if you are the lonely old lady—better known as the sugar mommy—then upgrade to being a cougar or panther. Then remember that this is the price you pay when you play with puppies. Eventually, they are going to lick you in the mouth. Make sure that he has all of his shots so that you don't finally get a gift from him that keeps on giving.

Give the babysitter a permanent position, since she spends most of the time with him anyway while you are out working. This is a time in your life when you know what you want, so go get it! Wake up and smell the coffee and stop drinking the Kool-Aid. Give this loser a one-way ticket to Disneyland and take yourself to Vegas. If you must play with something, try the one-armed bandit; at least there is a small chance you can win. File for custody of your life and get your passion back so that you can step into your victory.

༄

Conclusion

Once again, your gut is talking. Listen so you can throw away the antacids. Every woman needs a man, and every boy needs a *Madden NFL*. Is it possible that you suffer from low self-esteem? Whatever the case, it's time to step back and do some self-evaluation.

One of the most important parts of any relationship is the way the other person makes you feel. If your relationship makes you feel special and loved, then you probably are, and perhaps such a connection is feasible with some work. However, when you are in a relationship and you feel used or degraded, those feelings are there for a reason and should not go without being recognized. You are worthy of a man that is willing to earn your time and your love, and this one has not done either. It is impossible to be in a relationship by yourself. You are special, and there is someone out there who is willing to show you just how special you are. However, it is not possible for this to happen if Mr. Wrong is occupying the space rent free that should be reserved available for Mr. Right.

Change can be frightening but only by changing can you experience personal growth. A man's closest friends and peers are one of the very best windows into his mental and emotional world. Are his friends doing positive things with their lives and committed to living a good life? Does he have any married friends who have stable relationships where both partners are relatively happy and fulfilled? If you answered No to these questions, this is a good sign that he lacks maturity and therefore will be limited in a committed stable, relationship, at this time. Postpone your life and wait for this man to grow up, only if you believe in your heart that tomorrow will be promised to you. However, if you have come to believe that all you really have is today, don't take a rain check promising a healthy relationship tomorrow.

Today I will Release and Let Go of :

.

4

Mary Hippie, She's Harry's lady

~

Lying is a part of his everyday routine, but he really isn't good at it. When he's not getting high, he's getting low—real low. His pity parties are open invitations for you listen to how rough it is being an addict and how everything is completely out of his control. He has reached his ultimate goal if he can persuade you to support his habit. Your family members are ready to admit you to the nearest health facility, and you are on the threshold of suicide. His family members have sorrowfully disassociated themselves due to lack of trust and repeated trauma. You put up with his addiction because you know that you are all that he has left, and he reminds you of this every chance he gets.

Somehow, you have become his caretaker and enabler. When he's at his summer home (jail), he gets a chance to think and thank you for all that you have done and make a lot of promises. He knows exactly where he went wrong and vows to never touch the stuff again. He is desperate to demonstrate his love to you, and he needs a second chance so that he can show you when he gets out—because he certainly cannot lose you now, not at a time like this. In the meantime, you visit him in prison, handle all of his affairs, pay his bills, and take care of him and his children alone. He looks great now that he's been in jail and has lots of free time on his hands to improve himself, lifting weights, getting proper rest, and eating three farm meals a day.

Currently the dust has settled, and the fog has certainly had time to clear the air; therefore, the Jailbird has had nothing but time to figure out exactly how to convince you that he has had a spiritual awakening! When the door to the cage opens and it is finally your turn to find out why the caged bird sings, instead of flying to your nest, he decides he wants to spend just one more night with another dove and immediately flies south. You start the vicious cycle again.

∽⟋

Let's Talk

Get off that roller coaster and leave this guy in the amusement park. You are not Mary, although he may by all means be Harry. There is no need for you to feel bad about abandoning the relationship, because this guy checked out a long time ago—if he was ever even there. All this guy has left you with is a map of the amusement park he left you in, with a big, red X on the picture of the haunted house, better known as the House of Pain, with a legend reading "You are here." Try to find your way out, but only if you are willing to get run over by another derailed roller coaster!

There are lots of programs now available that offer help to the suffering addict and his family. Do not stay with an addict who does not want or think he needs help. Living with this type of addict is like living in hell. The only thing that he will do for you is keep the fire burning. He has built up a tolerance to the drugs, so he needs more, and you have built up a tolerance to him, so you allow more—get it?

You allow things to take place in your house and your life that you never imagined would be acceptable to you. You were once a law-abiding citizen who would never think of allowing drugs in your house, less so in your possession. He has lost control over his drug use, and you have lost control over your will to say no and over what you will allow in your domain. He may even want to stop, but he can't—not on his own. You may even want to kick him to the curb, but you can't—not on your own. There is a lot of shame and guilt that comes along with this addiction, so it is much easier for him to stay in a state of denial. To a certain degree, you stay in denial about a lot of things, too.

Blackouts really help this guy to live with himself because he has no memory of his behavior when he gets sober. As pieces of the day before begin to trickle back into his memory, he may become very depressed and paranoid. You stay depressed and paranoid because you never know what is going to happen. Don't be his victim. If you are going to suffer from the effects of drugs or alcohol, at least be a willing participant. This man is battling something that is bigger than the both of you. He is only interested in getting and using, and he will take you as a hostage if need be.

⌒౧

Conclusion

You have been in total denial about your loved one being an addict because of your hope that it was just a phase and not really anything to be concerned about. You have been keeping all of your emotions inside, often trying to keep the peace by pretending that your problems do not exist. You are living a vicious cycle that goes from minimizing the situation to lecturing, blaming, or criticizing the chemically dependent person. However, you take over all responsibilities of the addicted person; you cover for and pick up his slack to minimize any and all negative consequences.

This person can depend on you to repeatedly come to the rescue—bailing him out of jail and financial problems—or any situation that becomes unmanageable because of the addiction. He has become another dependent, and you treat him like a child. Perhaps there is something inside you that makes you enjoy taking care of your loved one, and you feel superior when you support him, even though he is an adult. There is also a certain amount of control you have when you deal with a person who is totally dependent on you, and this may be somewhat of a payoff. Conversely, there is no doubt that you are an enabler and should probably seek help for yourself as well, because you will not be able to stop accepting your loved one's lies, giving your loved one money, or making excuses for their behavior without help from an outside source. An enabler is someone who – usually unintentionally – helps to make a person's drug use problems and addictions possible by engaging in behaviors they mistakenly think will help the person. Does this sound at all familiar? Well in reality, the enabler only hurt their self as well as the addict.

When defining family roles in addiction, the Colorado State University describes the enabler: "The enabler is the person who allows substance abuse to continue by "saving" the abuser from the consequences of his or her actions. My question for the enabler is; once you have warned a person several times that the ship, is sinking and they refuse to get off; what do you expect to accomplish, by going down with the person, that has decided to stay on and the ship?

Continue this relationship only if you are willing to give this guy everything you own, including your dignity and possibly your life. You already know that he will stop at nothing to get what he wants, and if you get in the way, you will come face-to-face with immediate danger! Make no mistake: you are just as sick as he is. The only difference is that he medicates himself, and you do it all sober. Allow me to clarify: this means he may not have experienced quite as much pain as you've endured during the relationship process, because he was intoxicated while you were sober.

On the other hand, the light at the end of this tunnel does not have to be another oncoming train. You can survive this type of abuse if you are willing to do the work. Your chance of complete recovery is almost 100 percent. However, he is an addict for life and may continue the vicious cycle of jails and institutions until death. Some addicts make a complete recovery and start a new way of life. However, this new way of life may not include you. Once the fog of insanity has been lifted and reality sets in, the recovering addict may discover that you are not what he wants in a woman after all. You may be a constant reminder of the life he is trying to forget. You may even find this new guy arrogant and self-centered. The recovering addict will not be the same guy you fell in love with, which could be great—or really bad.

The guy you fell in love with does not exist; he was a figment of the addict's imagination, a character that the addict developed to appear somewhat normal. He worked really hard keeping this guy alive just for you, but this character is no longer needed. Now that he is recovering, he may not even remember that guy. This addict told you so many lies when he was under the influence that he may not know how to communicate with you sober. You are truly a stranger to the recovering addict, and it is very possible that he is a stranger to you. To make matters even worse, the recovering addict is even a stranger to himself. This guy will now try to get to know who he is, and you may be in his way. Many recovering addicts seek other recovering addicts as partners because they feel that they understand each other's struggle.

However, if this guy is an active participant in a twelve-step program and is willing to do the work, this may be a relationship worth holding on to. Once the insanity has lifted, the new life will emerge. The two of you may be able to resolve your differences and become a testimony for others who are still striving to find their new way of life. Remember, recovery is a one-day-at-a-time process. He didn't get this way overnight, and he won't recover by the next morning. Both of you have been victims of drug abuse and may require some outside help. Remember to keep the focus on yourself and never try to be someone else's if it means settling for a zero.

～⊙

Today I will Release and Let Go of :

5

Till Death Do Us Part

You have the perfect family: two girls, a boy, and a husband—although he is not drop-dead handsome, he makes a pretty decent living. When the two of you first met, he used to send flowers to you at work and surprise you by showing up without an invitation at places that he knew you would frequent. For instance, you would come out of a store and there he would be, standing in the parking lot next to your car. When you asked him how he knew you were there, he would say that he just happened to be passing by and saw your car. He was a guy that almost read your mind.

Early on in the relationship, you would catch him gazing at you while you were sleeping. In the beginning, whenever you talked, he would be all ears, and you found it truly intriguing that someone found your conversation so interesting. He wanted to know everything about you and all your associates. Before long, he was ready to move things to another level and commit to a serious relationship. He started by laying down the ground rules for what he thought a relationship should look like and what role a woman should play in it. One day, he told you that he never wanted to live without you and pulled out a ring.

29

People came from all over to celebrate this union, and you were the envy of many women's eyes. Shortly after the two of you were married, though, the honeymoon was over.

One day, the new puppy that he brought the children urinated on the floor, and he went into a full rage. Without notice, he grabbed the puppy and threw him into the wall and then out into the yard. The children were terrified, screaming, "Daddy, please stop," but he slung them off of him as if they were rag dolls, threw them out into the yard too, and closed the door. The next five hours were spent drilling you on how stupid you were and yelling, "Get up the piss before I throw it on you," and tossing furniture through the air. Now, the reason that he insisted that he must have at the bare minimum an acre of land around the house you bought has become very clear. He needed the privacy for what now feels like his torture chamber.

Right from the beginning, he was overly codependent to the point of being creepy and you are always tired because he keeps you up all night talking. He doesn't think your friends and family value you enough, or even at all. He demands so much of your time that you find yourself always explaining to people why you cannot go out with them. Although you enjoy the attention your anxiety soars if you're just a few minutes late, because you know how worried and upset he will be. Sometimes because of how easily he becomes annoyed when he doesn't know your whereabouts, you wonder if this is directly related to his childhood. The only thing that you know about his family is that he told you they were abusive and they have been estranged for many years.

As a direct result of him being abandoned as a child, he has great difficulty trusting strangers and chooses not to have any friends. To you, his past only goes back to the day you met him, and you are his only plans for the future. When you finally get the nerve to pack your bags to leave, he threatens to commit suicide and report you to child welfare, because he claims that you are a horrible mother and that the children are not properly taken care of.

You have been intentionally isolated from all of your family and friends, one at a time. Because of the influence of the Internet and cable on children, he has seen no need for any of those services in the home. You had a pretty good job when the two of you married, but he begged you to allow him to be the man of the house and fully support his family. You had always wanted to be a homemaker while your children were young anyway, so you put your career on the back burner to stay home with your family.

Now that you depend solely on this guy's income, your days are spent hearing how stupid, fat, and ugly you are. Dinner should be on the table when he gets home from work, and if it is not what he wants and the way he wants it, you, the children, the walls, and the floor get to wear it! You are home now where he can't watch you, so he constantly accuses you of being sneaky and unfaithful. You can't even go to the bathroom and close the door without him wondering if you are dating the toilet paper.

Although his bedroom manner is degrading and abusive, if you show any sign of rejecting him, it only makes matters worse, so you wait for him to finish so you can wash away the misery after he falls asleep. All of his shortcomings, character defects, and problems are suddenly your fault, because he has the weight of the entire family on his shoulders. Whenever he is around you get a sick feeling right in the pit of your stomach because you are afraid of what he may do. So you find yourself always trying to avoid certain topics, out of fear of angering him. Being criticized and put down has become part of your daily routine. Lately, you can't do anything right in his opinion and as a result you provoke him to anger constantly. You are starting to feel like a piece of property or a sex object, instead of a person.

In an effort to weather the storm, you start drinking to numb the pain of emotional injuries that have gone without treatment and thinking about the severity of your situation. Alcohol is sometimes used daily by both of you as a means of escape from the everyday reality of this toxic relationship; however, it is like throwing water on a grease fire.

You stay and put up with the abuse because you have now been forbidden to get a job and therefore lack the financial independence you need to leave. Emotional abuse has taken its toll, and your lack of social support helps your partner to control you. Shame keeps you from contacting friends, family, and the outside world about your dilemma. Isolation has become your prison without bars. You have been humiliated so much by him in front of people that you isolate yourself voluntarily so that you don't have to worry about his mood swings and public embarrassment. Your soul cries out to be restored, but it falls on deaf ears.

Eventually, he starts using threats of physical attack to keep you in a state of perpetual fear and tells you that if you attempt to destroy his family by leaving, he can and will kill you. Somehow, you feel that perhaps the violence is temporary or caused by unusual circumstances; you even start to blame yourself. You think about how great things were in the beginning and somehow begin to wonder if you or perhaps the pressures of work or his sad childhood have something to do with what has happened. Could any of it be responsible for his actions? And the cycle of domestic violence continues.

Subsequently, after a violent episode, he has no problem performing a four-alarm cry in front of you to prove how passionate he is. However, if you allow yourself to look straight through the tears into his eyes, the tunnels to his soul, you will discover that this man is empty on the inside. The telltale sign of his emptiness is the fact that he is trying to fill himself up with you.

∽੭

Let's Talk

Often, when facing consequences, abusers will beg for forgiveness and promise to change. They may even mean what they say in the moment, but their true goal is to stay in control and keep you from leaving the isolation camp that for some reason, you've almost managed to escape. Most of the time, the abuser will return to abusive behavior once he feels that the threat of abandonment is no longer on the table and he has been forgiven.

Although you may think you're the only one who understands him or feel responsible to fix his problems, by staying and accepting repeated abuse, you're only reinforcing and enabling the abusive behavior. Most abusers have psychological issues and must be willing to first take full responsibility for their behavior and stop blaming you and others for their shortcomings. They should seek professional treatment.

You need to know that the abuse that you suffered at his hands was never your fault at any time or place. Never accept any responsibility for abusive behavior that's been inflicted on you. Even if the abuser gets counseling or attends a program for batterers, there is no guarantee that he will change or that the abuse will not happen again. Make your decision to be with this person based on the person he is now, not on the man you want him to be.

Try not to allow the fear of the unknown, such as what your abusive partner will do where you'll go, or how you'll support yourself or your children, paralyze you. Instead, focus on what you do know now: things will not get any better if you don't make an attempt to rescue yourself. In fact, there is a very good chance you may not make it out alive if you don't. Start with a small step, like breaking the code of silence that you have internally vowed to maintain, and soon you will be walking into your victory! Take a deep breath, because you already know what to do. If not, continue to read. I promise you that I will not finish this chapter until you do know.

Wake up, girlfriend! If you are not dead, then why are you letting him bury you alive? Emotional abuse can leave your self-esteem deflated, and when this happens, at this point you can feel that your self-worth is low or gone. However, you don't get to blame this on anyone but yourself, because you are the only one who can maintain your self-esteem—that's why they call it self-esteem. You are not a door mat and you certainly don't deserve to be treated like one. Take a deep breathe, get up, dust yourself off and find the strength to reclaim your life.

Self-confidence cannot be taken away from you, because it is the way that you feel about yourself. Now, you can credit him for treating you like you're nothing, but you must take all of the credit if you stay and continue to allow this type of destruction to damage your character. Don't depend on anyone to repair your self-esteem; this is a task that you must complete on your own for it to be real. Now, it is possible for someone to boost your self-esteem, but this is just a temporary fix. After this guy, girlfriend, you don't need a hotshot; you need a new battery.

Have you ever observed that when you are very happy with yourself and your life, men seem to notice you from afar? The moment that you get engaged, the whole world seems to find you attractive, and you meet a guy who you would love to date you if you were single. Old boyfriends remember that you are still alive and start ringing your phone off the hook, begging you for a second chance. Your family and friends tell you over and over how much you are glowing lately.

But here, you have been living a lie, pretending to be happy. This guy has made you feel uncomfortable right from the start, when he began to change your life style immediately. You made a conscious decision to dismiss numerous gut feeling in the beginning of the relationship. You witnessed several flares going off warning you that this man was not being authentic right from the start of the relationship. It became your mission to make sure that no one else could see what you already saw but refused to acknowledge. Therefore, you were OK with being isolated because you were able to help him hide the fact that he was strange—to say the least—from your friends and loved ones. Eventually, you found yourself afraid to let people know that you were now in a hopeless, helpless situation, especially if it wasn't your first. Suddenly, you are withdrawn from your family and friends because Mr. Can't live without you has drained you dry. You have been in a total state of denial right from the beginning and eventually lost the ability to listen to your own instincts.

This guy is like a time bomb and is ready to explode without notice. You have been subjected to a lot of trauma that has made you fragile; therefore, you will need a bomb squad to help you to get away properly. Your "bomb squad" is your support network, something you'll need to develop with perhaps a neighbor or close friend. You'll need to set up coded signals that allow you to let your network know when you need help without alarming your tormentor. Something like turning on the porch light could mean

"Help Call police." Let people know what is going on in your life. Find a safe place to go without further delay. Get in touch with the police department in your area and find out what resources are available to you and your family. Don't stop screaming "Help!" until you have found it. Time is something that you don't have. Seek help today. Don't even finish this book until you have rescued yourself.

Conclusion

You are unique and worthy of being recognized. You have contributions to make to this world, and you can't make them if you are no longer in it. Get yourself someone you can have a partnership with. Remember, true love should never make you feel frightened, alarmed, or worried. If you are constantly walking on eggshells because you are afraid that you will make your husband or mate angry, then you need to think seriously about planning your exit. Why eggshells? Because your gut is telling you that you are living with a time bomb! Don't wait for this person to completely lose all control explode and make you a statistic. As the author of your life story it is imperative that you recognize when it is time to place a period, question mark or start a new chapter. When you KNOW, What you KNOW, What you KNOW, place a period, where you had the question mark and move on with your life. Every book has several chapters and your life story is no different. Some chapters in your life will be all-inclusive and comparable to the previous chapters. Regrettably, there will be characters in your life story that are dear to you and you will not be able to imagine, writing your life story without them included in it.

Although it is your life story and you are the author, not everyone is met to move on to the next chapter of your life. Some people will be written out of your life story. When this comes to the light it will be your responsibility as the author, to re-event your life's story, while accepting the things that you cannot change and to recognize the difference. Just as not everyone is predestined to move on to the next chapter of your life, as you go through life on lifes terms it will sometimes become crucial for you to make a conscious decision, to write some people, places and things out of your life story; for various reasons. There are some people that you may have written into your life story that were hypothetically just passing through. Take the time to write out anyone or anything that you know in your heart, should not be occupying space in your head or your life story, at this time. Never attempt to artificially in-simulate someone into your life that should not be there. Do yourself a favor and erase any desires that you have for anyone to be in your life that is unavailable to you, because they are unavailable for a reason. Now that you have the clean pages in your life story available to use, you are free to start a new chapter!

There are many support groups and programs available online that can give you step-by-step advice and support on how to flee a toxic relationship without incident. Consider doing a search online for battered and abused women support groups in your area. Know what all your options are and pursue them. If you have never been physically abused by a mental and emotional abuser, then don't wait around until you are, because your time is running out. Never consider yourself lucky that he has only verbally abused you and has never been physically abusive, because physical abuse can stop, but verbal abuse can and will scar you for life!

A Free Flyer from The National Center for Victims of Crime has been provided at the end of this book with information for people that are victims of domestic abuse.

Today I will Release and Let Go of :

6

If Being the Side Chick Is Wrong, I Don't Want to Be Right

~

Although you have a lot to be grateful for, your life was dreary and empty until he came along. You wore all the best perfumes but seldom had anyone around who bothered to smell them. Now, the perfume really isn't necessary because he loves you naturally, just the way you are. Besides, you really don't want to risk the chance of sending him home smelling like perfume or smudged with makeup, anyway. He is kind, considerate, passionate, loveable—and married. You feel like this guy is trustworthy because he was honest with you right from the start. He never tried to hide the fact that he was married, and when you asked him if he had children, he explained to you that his kids were the only reason that he was still with her.

He is your secret lover and his wish is your command. He came into your life when you thought your chance of having a healthy, stable relationship, was bleak because of past failures. You two seemed to be attracted to each other right from the start. It is almost as if you two were destined to be together. This guy seemed like he was made for you. The two of you never argue and really appreciate every moment that you get the opportunity to share.

He filled up a space in your life that was empty until he came along, and now you feel like it has meaning. He loves you just the way you are. Your only problem is his wife. Why do you get all of the tough breaks? Who gave this woman this wonderful man? Clearly, she does not deserve him. He's definitely your soul mate! You are the woman of his dreams. You are always ready to listen to his problems, and, unlike his wife, you turn him on so much that he attacks you the moment he sees you. I mean, this man and his wife haven't slept together in years! The only reason he didn't leave five years ago, when he first met you, was because he was waiting for the kids to get older. Now that the kids are older, they need him more than ever, though, so he still can't leave.

He did try to tell his wife he was leaving, but that's when she announced that her health was failing. This was really the straw that broke the camel's back. How dare she be so dependent on this man! This woman is probably the most self-centered, inconsiderate, codependent woman alive. You, on the other hand, would have been a real helpmate instead of a total dependent. She rarely even cooks him a decent meal after a hard day's work. The only reason he has gained so much weight since you have been together is because of those good, home cooked meals you've been providing. His wife was once a beautiful woman, but after she had the kids, she just let herself go. You, on the other hand, always look so sexy that he just can't keep his hands off you—beside the fact that you are ten years younger.

In the beginning, he was able to get away to see you all the time. Now this thing that he married can't seem to do anything without him. He has a nice Mercedes, but when he visits you, he always drives the old car because it is less noticeable. The poor guy has put everything that he has worked so hard for on the line to spend time with you. If he was ever caught cheating on her, she would take him for everything he owns and disgrace him in front of his entire family. Just when the two of you managed to get some time together on Sunday mornings, his wife decided to join a church and started nagging and complaining about him not going with her and the kids. So now, to stop his wife from nagging, he's at church with the family, and those romantic, stolen Sunday mornings that the two of you used to have are now a thing of the past. Need I go any further? Does any of this sound familiar?

⁓つ

Let's Talk

Girlfriend, please catch the next spaceship back to Earth, because the only thing that you are right about so far is the two of you deserving each other. This man has had you singing "(If Loving You Is Wrong) I Don't Want to Be Right" from the very beginning. Get a life, or at least get a man of your own. This man has his cake and is eating it, too. You may think that you have the best of both worlds because you don't have to deal with the children and the household chores, but you have been in denial from the very beginning. You have denied the fact that he is married. He took a vow to love this woman for better or worse, through sickness and in health. I can't say that he has broken this vow completely, because he is still there. How can you love someone who is so disrespectful and constantly lying to someone that he took a vow to love?

Although she is being betrayed and deceived, this woman has the total package. You, on the other hand, have a few stolen moments, a wet behind, and a lot of lonely days and nights to look forward to. While you were eating alone on Thanksgiving, wondering what he was doing, did it ever dawn on you that he was actually enjoying himself, sitting at the head of the dinner table, thanking God for his wonderful family, and complimenting his beautiful wife on how wonderful the food was? While you were alone on Christmas, looking at the lights on the tree with his gift still lying under it, listening to "It Will Be a Blue Christmas Without You," he was presenting his wife with the most beautiful piece of jewelry, hoping to relieve his guilty conscience for all of those times that he cheated on her. Hiding has to be exhausting and humiliating, not to mention a real damper on your self-esteem.

Remember when he told you years ago that he would leave his wife when his kids were old enough to understand? Now That the kids are older, his excuse to stay with his wife is because she cannot control the kids alone. Wake up, girlfriend.

Stop kidding yourself. This man found time for you in the beginning, and he can still find time for you now if he wants it. Do you think that it is at all possible that when he doesn't come to visit you, he is trying to do the right thing at home? A man will be with the woman of his desires regardless of his present situation. If your married man fits this profile, more than likely, he will never leave his wife. Now, in some rare cases, the "other woman" is able to convince the man she is the better one, and he does leave his wife and family. Or the wife somehow catches on to the affair and throws the husband out.

No matter how he ends up leaving, though, deep down inside, if he has any conscience or if he took any of his marriage vows seriously and any part of him is at least human, he will always wonder if he did the right thing. His guilt will eat at him like a cancer and many times prompt him to run back to his wife like a firefighter running into a burning building with a little old lady standing on the rooftop!

It won't take him long to realize that the grass at your house still has to be cut and that you don't wake up looking like Ms.

America either. You suffer from PMS worse than his wife, and you used to look so good to him, but now you spend too much money on hair and clothes. Don't be so hard on this poor guy because of the sudden change in his appearance. You have been wondering why he never takes time to groom himself anymore. What happened to the guy who was always immaculately dressed? Not to mention the pair of disgusting-looking underwear you found lying on the bathroom floor. Oh, that's right, his dirty underwear would be a total surprise to you because you never had to wash them or pick them up before! Well, I guess he never told you that his wife picked out all of his clothes, and he hasn't dressed himself since he got married. All those nice shirts you like, his wife picked out because she liked them, too.

As far as the shave, his wife hated his beard because it irritated her. It took her many years to get him to shave daily, but he doesn't have to worry about her nagging him about that now. And when did he start drinking every night? Oh, right: most nights, you weren't with him. Long story short, honey: you don't know this man. You fell in love with someone else's husband. Those two married people were as one—a lot of the things that you liked so much about him were a direct result of her. You wanted her husband, so take his dirty underwear as part of the package.

Have you ever heard of "rebound"? Well, this, I am afraid, is you. That cologne he wears that you love so much? His wife bought that for him. This poor guy didn't own any cologne until he met her. She put up with this man's shortcomings and immaturity until he became husband-worthy, and now you seem to think he was born that way and made for you. A lot of the things that seem so wonderful about this guy are because he lived with his wife for so long. He would never leave the toilet seat up because he was already potty trained and housebroken, but occasionally, he will forget to take out the trash.

Very few relationships that create so much pain result in something long lasting. This guy may not go back to his wife, but it is not likely that you will be his next. I hate to tell you this, but he probably does not look at you as wife material. Your title was "the other woman," and chick on the side does not usually meet wife requirements. There is a whole different set of rules to follow for that. You see, the more time that you spend with a person, the more is revealed. Your time with this man was strategically planned.

His spouse was not the only one left in the dark about a lot of things. More than likely, he lied to you just as much as—if not more than—he lied to her. Think about how often he told you that his wife was great in bed the night before or that the kids weren't home all weekend and they went out on a "date night." Nobody subjects themselves to misery twenty-four hours a day. Believe me, there were some good times that were not mentioned. Perhaps when he told you on several occasions that someone was sick or in the hospital, and as a result he was missing for days and neglected to call, and you believed he was telling the truth. Have you ever thought that he could have been on a family vacation, having the time of his life with his wife?

It isn't my intention to hurt you or make you feel bad. All right, I lied. I *have* tried to make you feel bad, because you should. You have been in total denial about this guy—and about your part as a home wrecker as well. You need to call the relationship the two of you are having what it is: an adulterous affair. What you have been doing is wrong, all wrong. Ask the God of your understanding for forgiveness, and then forgive yourself. You are worthy of undivided love and a family of your own.

The next time a married guy gives you his gloom-and-doom story, tell him to hang in there and run as fast as you can. Never let married man cry on your shoulder, because his head will soon fall down to your breast. Tell that grown man to go get a bottle, and stop breastfeeding him. Kneel down, dust yourself off, and when you finish, stand up and put your head to the sky. Smell the fresh air and start your life anew. The man for you will not be found in someone else's home, fathering and nurturing someone else's children or lying in someone else's arms. If you are looking in any of these places, you will never find him, love, or happiness.

Don't walk away as a self-proclaimed home wrecker—or an accomplice. You knew this man was not on the available list, and you laid in wait like a stalker for him to sneak about. In some states, you would be considered just as guilty as him and would get the same penalty if the crime were murder. Yes, I used the word *murder*, because it is the killing of a union of two people who were joined that no one was supposed to take apart. That's right; you helped change the hands of time. Therefore, everything that this union was presumed to bring to the universe was aborted.

~⊙

Conclusion

Regardless, if you are, "the main chick" or "the side chick", both chicks are being plucked, by the same rooster. You have been disrespected, lied to, and deceived, regardless of what side of the bed he has been sleeping with you on. Allow me to determine your positions; if you are not the main woman, and you are expected to be comfortable with zero plans for the two of you for the future, never mention his wife and/or main woman. Anticipate frequent changes in plans, without notice; Focus only on stolen moments that are spent together. If any of these terms and conditions sound comparable to the relationship that you currently hold in your man's life, then you are perhaps the chick on the side, better known as "the side chick." Most side chicks have been informed to never attempt to communicate with the main chick in any way. If a side chick should contact the main chick – her side chick positon will be terminated immediately, indefinitely.

Many wives almost instantaneously view the side chick as an opponent, invading her territory, in a competition and the husband assumes the status of a trophy. The side chick becomes the wife's highest priority of consideration. In the interim the fraudulent, manipulative behavior of the spouse, will be placed on the back burner, for future reference. Nevertheless, many wives that are victims of infidelity, miserably fail to acknowledge, a well-known fact; the side chick has not made any commitment to love them exclusively. The spouse has represented himself deceptively, the entire time, with both women. Unfortunately, the wife may think she is winning the battle by getting rid of the side chick however she may ultimately lose the war, because she will never be able to change, what she declines to acknowledge.

If you are the side chick and for some strange reason he leaves the main woman to remain with you, how will you be able to trust, an untrustworthy man, like this? What makes you think he will not replace "the side chick" with yet another side chick? There are no guarantees about the outcome of a relationship with a man that is a cheater at heart; he will not change unless he wants to do it. Until that happens, if you are promoted to the main chick, please know that eventually another sidepiece may fill the vacancy, which you've left behind.

Start cleaning your house now and when true love knocks at your door, you will be available to open it. Your willingness to seek closure for what is wrong, shall eventually lead you to the desires of your heart. Get up in the morning and talk out loud to the god of your understanding. Speak what you are expecting into existence and aggressively seek it. Birth something or someone that can be yours into your life. You are responsible for your own happiness. Change can be frightening, but only by changing will you experience what has been unwearyingly, waiting for you, on the other side of the mountain there will be daylight!

Envision the universe as a large canvas and you are the artist painting a picture of the road that you traveled, for the cover of your life story. As the author of your life story you will find there are many ordinary roads to travel however all of the ordinary roads will lead you to the same ordinary people, places and things. The ordinary roads have lots of ordinary company along the way and can be walked naturally within your comfort zone, with very little exertion. The only other option is the mountain that merely a few select people, appear to be climbing. The mountain is steep and there are many slopes and valleys. Although very few people have the courage to climb the mountain, the only requirement is to have a dream and the passion to fuel the unyielding determination to make that dream come true! Nevertheless if you reach the top of the mountain, you will be able to see the other side of ordinary and know that it is extraordinary! The decisions that you make today, will ultimately affect your tomorrow.

Today I will Release and Let Go of :

7

I Just Don't Want to Be Lonely

OK, so he doesn't have a job, but he is a great cook! There are absolutely no worries about what's for dinner at your house, providing you have supplied the ingredients.

A good friend of yours who was always complaining about her brother being a freeloader and wanting to get him out of her house neglected to tell you that he was drop-dead gorgeous. One day, you were visiting your girlfriend, and a guy with the most pleasant voice walked into the room and insisted that he be introduced to you. After a brief encounter in your girlfriend's kitchen, you invited him to your house—and your house quickly became his home, sweet home.

Although your girlfriend, his sister, gave you a fair warning about his character defects, you find him to be great company and a welcome change to an empty house with four walls that you felt were beginning to close in on you. Besides, he seemed to be a pretty good guy and not a bad fixer-upper project. With a little work and a lot of money, you manage to get his teeth done, wardrobe adjusted, self-esteem renewed, and old girlfriend back on the chase.

Suddenly, a man whose only means of survival was his sister is now quite the ladies' man. You find yourself spending countless days and nights alone and have finally admitted that you really are alone. One day while hanging out at the mall, trying to pass time, to your surprise, you come across your ex-husband, who is in town for a visit but is seriously considering relocating. Nothing has changed about him; he still has that thing he had when you decided to marry him. He is really happy to see you and anxious to pick up where the two of you had left off. You go home and quickly pack your girlfriend's brother's bags. You drive by her house and toss the bags in front of it.

Later that night, you have candlelight dinner with your ex-husband, and he spends the evening. The next morning, he seems to be in a hurry and explains that he'll see you later that night. You rush out to get your hair and nails done and hurry back to clean the house and prepare one of his favorite meals. When daylight turns to night, you decide to call but only get voice mail. So you open a bottle of wine, play some of your old love songs, and wait. After numerous walks to the window, several bottles of wine, and countless unanswered calls, you decide to curl up on the couch and go to sleep with your head resting on one hand, attempting to preserve what was once a fabulous hairdo worn just for him. Three days go by without even a glimmer of hope that he would even think of coming back.

It's Christmas Eve, it's snowing outside, and there is a knock at the door. It's your girlfriend's brother! He hasn't brought any gifts, but he actually looks pretty good, and he sure beats a blank. You open up a bottle of wine, and the two of you have a white Christmas, complete with your chestnuts roasting on an open fire, and he is enjoying the luxuries of your nice, warm home. The next day, he goes to the kitchen to see what you might have purchased and prepares breakfast for the both of you in bed.

As you're lying in each other's arms, he tells you how distraught he was when you asked him to leave. Suddenly, there is a knock at the door. It's your ex-husband. He has his bags in the car and can explain everything.

૮–૭

Let's Talk

You have given numerous men permission to rack up frequent flyer miles with you. They're in and out of your life through the revolving door to your house. Your assortment of men is more diverse than the selection at the local convenience store. Your house should be your sanctuary, yet it has become a shelter for any gentleman or whoever could come anywhere close to being a companion that cares to hang his hat for the evening. Your guests find no need to rush back or reserve a room at your place, because the doors are always open. You're willing to settle for whatever excuse that is given providing it does not necessitate you to spend another night feeling alone.

૮–૭

Conclusion

At first glance, it may appear you're only interested in making sure that you don't have an empty pillow beside you at night. However, when we look deeper, it becomes quite apparent that a woman like this is very uncomfortable with herself. When a woman suffers from low self-esteem, it's very easy for her to commit herself to anyone who may express interest in her, regardless of how she may feel about him. Often, women suffering from this issue feel that they have to put up with behavior from men that don't satisfy them and consider themselves lucky to have a man at all. Many times, when a woman has low self-esteem, she appears obsessed and infatuated, and this is a toxic cocktail for any relationship. A relationship should never be artificially moved along and most men run from Fatal Attractions.

When your timing in a relationship is unrealistic and you make things happen, this will ultimately open up doors for deception and rejection. Because you don't see yourself as lovable, you feel like you have to settle for anything just to have someone. Unfortunately, this can make you very easily become infatuated with anyone that appears willing to show you any type of attention, including negative attention and you will consider it to be affection. When this happens, you are instantly ready to form a committed relationship. You're already so far ahead in your mind that when the relationship doesn't develop easily or on your timeline, it's hard to tolerate. However, instead, of accepting it for what it is, you think that this is your cue to work even harder at making it happen.

You are familiar with being left, being cheated on, etc. – you gravitate toward relationships in which you're able to feel this familiar insecurity. When it's not there, you may even create it. If the relationship becomes too secure, you may become disinterested and bored and you may stray. You have become so accustomed to saving an insecure relationship that insecure relationships become the only ones that you unknowingly gravitate toward. You find yourself willing to commit yourself to anyone who expresses interest in you. You may even be willing to put up with behavior that doesn't satisfy you, even though you know that you are not happy and deserve better, you continue to settle for less. Be your authentic self and stop pretending to be happy. Learn to say NO, you will be able to accomplish this mission simply by letting your yes mean yes and a no mean NO! Say what you mean and mean what you say. Give yourself permission to admit that you made a mistake, diagnose the lesson that the mistake taught you, forgive yourself, forgive everyone involved. Move on with your life you are human and mistakes will happen. Take the opportunity to learn from all mistakes and turn it into personal growth. Stop beating yourself up over failed relationships and learn from them. Know that it is your reaction to your failures that will define you, not the failure. Start taking responsibility for your actions and accept them as a consequence of your choices. Focus on repair and how you can change things to make them more acceptable.

If you often find yourself trying to explain everything, such as why you're not pretty enough, smart enough or good enough, then that is an indicator of low self-esteem. Learn to accept compliments without trying to analyze the meaning behind the compliment. Know that you are wonderfully made and worthy to be praised.

Stop constantly trying to find ways to connect what is happening in the present to something that happened in the past. Focus on the here and now of your relationship. Learn how to treat yourself with respect and respect your partner. Avoid the fear of losing the other person and becoming jealous or paranoid over nothing. Never be afraid to reinvent yourself because positive change is growth. Very few things in life are met to stays the same. If you are the same this year, as you were last year, this is a good indication that you are not growing. Remove anyone or anything that is not conducive to your growth and you will find a person inside of you; that you always wanted to be.

When a person loves their self they will not tolerate rudeness, verbal abuse or any unacceptable behavior, directed towards them. Take off the mask that you have been wearing and allow people to accept you as your authentic self. Reveal your true feeling and you will know that you are loved and accepted for you, when the moment presents itself.

Men are naturally drawn and attracted to women who accept themselves. You must first be comfortable in your own skin before you can expect someone else to admire it. We teach people how to treat us, by the way that we treat ourselves. Give yourself the gift of self-love today and you will find that you are very loveable to others, tomorrow.

Know that you are lovable and worthy of being loved. Start with loving yourself. You will know when you have accomplished this very special task, because you will enjoy spending time alone. Never create the man of your dreams, because he will be just that: a dream. When you wake up, he could be a nightmare.

Today I will Release and Let Go of :

8

Jailbird Lover

~

You lie in bed and talk on telephone every night. You cannot wait until the doors to the Jailhouse opens for visitation. The opportunity to gaze through the glass at him weekly is just enough to keep hope alive. He is extremely good-looking, soft spoken and well built. Any woman would very easily be smitten with a man of his appearance under normal circumstances. You almost wonder why he is even interested in you because he appears so together for someone incarcerated. Your life has not been easy, and you are hoping that he is the missing piece of the puzzle. So far, things have been great; the two of you seem to have no complaints. He makes you feel like you are loved and needed. You spend countless hours on the phone with him daily, and he is always interested in what you are doing and wearing, where you are going, who you are talking to, and who you are with.

You never dreamed that you would fall deeply in love with a detainee also known as "Inmate 15263379," but it happened. Life is full of surprises, and this was one of them. Family and friends are trying to convince you to run while this bird is still in the cage, but you feel almost like a part of you is in there with him. So you do everything that a good jailhouse wife does. You spend weekends visiting the prison and evening waiting by the phone, for his call. Food has become your companion and you are not wearing the extra pounds that it rewards you with very well.

～シ

Let's Talk

There are many reasons a woman may end up involved with a man who is not available to her—or should I say, a man who is in jail? One of the reasons could be that she was already involved with this guy before he got locked up and she now feels that it is her duty, to take care of all of his needs as well as wants, while he is serving time in prison.

The rules for this type of journey are really simple. We all make mistakes and everyone deserves a second chance. This, dear, is very true, but let's first define the word mistake. "I made a mistake and forgot to file my taxes" is very different from "I made a mistake and robbed a bank." And, "I had too much to drink, and as a result I made a foolish decision and drove my vehicle" and "I needed money, so I sold drugs" are in two totally different ballparks. Got the picture? So you were already involved with this guy and he managed to make a mistake— or was even accused of a crime that he did not commit. What do you do? Well, first you look at the mistake. Was it really a mistake, or was it something premeditated and with malicious intent?

Ask yourself the following questions:
- ∾ Is this guy a repeat offender?
- ∾ Did this man bring harm to someone else?
- ∾ Was his crime a deliberate, malicious act that you are ashamed of?

- Did he hide what he was doing from you?
- Did his crime involve a child?
- Is he being charged as a sex offender?
- Was your relationship already at its end?
- Is this a man a habitual liar?
- Do you feel in your gut like he is a career criminal and will never change?
- Are you afraid of him?
- Is he expecting you to fully support him financially while he is in prison?

If you answered yes to any of the above questions, then leave the relationship while this bird is in the cage.

Today is precious: never take it for granted, because tomorrow is not promised to you. This man being locked up may be one of the best things that could ever have happened to you. If at all possible, plan your escape now and move before he gets out, leaving no forwarding address. You don't have to completely dispose of him all at once, but don't be converted into his cellmate. This guy can be like a drug, and you may find yourself taken into custody trying to capture that long-gone feeling from when he first swept you off your feet.

Don't listen to his family and friends when they try to persuade you to hold on to this nightmare, saying that you are all that he has. If he's worth holding on to, then how come he doesn't have them, too? These people are sick and tired of this repeat offender; they have come to the conclusion that he is just not worth the visit or the price of the phone call. But they feel sorry for him, and it relieves their consciences knowing that he has someone like you to run all the errands, buy all his clothes, send him money, and listen to his sad love song on the telephone. They have heard it all before and have pretty much chalked this guy up as a lost cause! Jump on the bandwagon and take away the keys to your heart.

Now, in some cases, the judicial system has failed, and an innocent man gets sentenced for a crime that he didn't commit, or a person is served undue justice in some way. If you know that to be true for this man and you were in a committed relationship with him, please take this into consideration before you jump ship. I am not by any means saying that because you were involved with him, this makes you the captain that should go down with the ship. However, if you are still in love with him and you feel he has been served undue justice, ask yourself the following questions:

- Would he wait for you if you were serving time in prison?
- Was your relationship in good standing before he went to prison?
- Are you married to this man?
- Do you love him?
- Are you fully aware of the circumstances of the crime that he is being charged for?
- Is this man worth waiting for?
- Can the two of you restore your lives when the doors to the prison are unlocked?
- Will he ever be able to join society again?
- Do you feel that he is worth waiting for, while he is serving time in prison?
- Did you enjoy any of the proceeds from the crime that he is serving time for?
- Do you feel like you are guilty, too?

If you have answered yes to three or more of the above questions, then perhaps you should seriously consider being there for this guy. Most definitely if you feel that you share some guilt and shared some of the proceeds from the crime that he is now being incarcerated for.

If you love this man and you know that he is innocent, he has already been let down by a system that was supposed to protect him. He does not need to be abandoned by a woman he loves and who says she loves him. Remember, we all fall down, but somehow, one day, if we're still alive, we get up!

Do what you can do to help this guy, but don't sacrifice yourself as a love offering. You will know when it gets to be too much for you to stomach and if you need to move on, because you will feel it in your gut. Nothing beats a failure but a try, and a try is all you can do at this time.

If you can't wait, don't beat yourself up. Not all love is strong enough to endure this type of separation, and not everyone that we love is meant to go on into the next chapter of our lives. Follow your gut and don't hold yourself hostage. True love is easy and done without remorse or regret. Nothing or no one worth waiting for should be an endless battle. You must take this relationship one day at a time, or if that is too long, one minute at a time. After a year, revisit the situation and look for noticeable change—not just in him, but in you. If you now look like a prisoner in love while he is the picture of health, you may have to free yourself. But if the two of you have grown closer because of this experience and you are both willing to consider a new way of life when he returns to society, then by all means, proceed.

Although this man might seem like the love of your life—on paper. Let's face facts: you don't know this guy. How can you know a person when you have never even walked down the street with him? Have you ever heard people say that you don't know a person until you have lived with him or her? Well, you will under no circumstances know what a person is capable of until you eliminate the shackles and the barbed wire fence. I am not saying that he is not in love with you and that your feelings about him are not genuine, but I am saying that you have'nt been given the opportunity to effectively be acquainted with him and vice versa.

Can you answer any of the following questions?

- ☙ What side of the bed does he like to sleep on (and does it matter)?
- ☙ Do you know his friends or associates who are still in his life today?
- ☙ Does he have good people skills?
- ☙ Are his feet cold at night?
- ☙ Is he good company on rainy days?
- ☙ Would he be willing to put his life on hold for you?
- ☙ Does he feel like society owes him something?
- ☙ Is he able to fulfill his promises?
- ☙ Does he take care of his personal hygiene?
- ☙ Is he an honest person and he fully self-supporting when he is not imprisoned?
- ☙ Does he cheat or flirt with every woman who walks by?
- ☙ Does he get along well with your friends and family?.   .
- ☙ Are the bars in his cell the only thing that is keeping him sober or from committing another crime?
- ☙ Is he gay or on the down low?

These are all very simple questions, and none of the answers to them indicate that a woman knows a man, but if she is in a devoted relationship, she should know the answers with some degree of accuracy. But if you're involved with a Jailbird, you can't answer any of the above questions, because you have never been acquainted with this man when he was not being told when to eat, sleep, bathe, and shave.

They have bars in jail, but none that he would want to frequent, and it is not likely that he would want to stay until they closed. More than likely, he is currently being fully subsidized by you—and the state—so you have no idea if he can even support himself. You will by no means be able to tell if this man is a flirt or has wandering eyes by looking at him in a visiting room. It has probably never entered your mind that he spends all day and half of the night thinking of what he is going to say on the telephone or in the visiting room to entertain you. Have you ever heard it said that to know him is to love him? Honey, this statement is very true, and you don't really know him.

~◦

Conclusion

This chapter is filled with questions that only you can answer. Give yourself the right to answer them honestly and sincerely. Any false answers can and will be used against you in your own conscience and should indicate that you are not interested in the truth about your situation, even if it happens to be coming from a very reliable source (yourself). Self-help is the best help for you at this time in your life. Be honest with yourself.

For some reason, you have put up a wall of defense in your life, and you refuse to allow anyone who you think can hurt you to penetrate it. This relationship is a liaison that is convenient, scheduled, monitored, and feels secure. You have elected a man who has no choice but to show you his good qualities and you feel like this is a safe and sound, meaningful link. This connection to you is fail proof. You don't have to worry about him leaving for another woman, because deep down inside, you know not many women are interested in dating a detainee.

The two of you are both prisoners in love—provided that he is in love. Chances are that he is just in need, and there is a big difference between being in love and being in need. You may not have figured it out, but this gentleman definitely needs you in his life right now, and that is all right. The question is will he still have the same necessity for you to be in his life, when the door of the cage has been opened? If you put a bird in a cage and you are this bird's only link to the outside world, the bird will depend on you for anything and everything that is going to make its stay in the cage more comfortable. The bird may even find ways to entertain you and show you that he cares. However, once the door to the cage has been opened and the bird has use of his wings, then it is very likely he may feel the need to fly south. It is very probable that this is where the term jailbird came from. The good part about this type of relationship is that you don't have to agonize about where he is at night, and you can feel pretty confident about what he is doing during the day.

Have you taken a look at your self-esteem lately? (Have you even considered looking at yourself lately?) Time is too precious to waste, despite his reassuring you how much you mean to him. This gentleman is not truly able to commit to a legitimate relationship with you at this time, but if you are willing to take the chance and you don't lose your self-respect over it for settling for such a lonely, practically nonexistent relationship, then by all means proceed, but with caution. This man may tell you that he loves you and may even have grown to do so, but at some point, he is going to have trouble respecting you as a woman for being so vulnerable to a practical stranger with nothing to proposition but shortcomings.

Chances are you feel like this man is the best that you can get for justifications that only you can distinguish. Well, flip a coin on this one. There is a small chance that you have stumbled upon true love that is just inaccessible at this time but will one day be your dream come true. The other side of the coin is that tomorrow is not promised to you. All you really have is today, and you have decided to spend that day waiting for someone who can only plan for tomorrow. So if you take a rain check for today with hopes of cashing in later, only to find out that you are not on tomorrow's schedule is this guy still worth waiting for? If you can answer yes to that question, then you, in my opinion, have taken this decision into the fullest consideration and are very well aware of the uncertain consequences of the choice you've been willing to make. Providing that you are of sound mind, then that is your choice. Life is truly all about choices and taking chances, and it seems that this is what you are doing: making a choice and taking a chance. Good luck.

~⊙

Today I will Release and Let Go of :

9

The Cougar and Her Cub

~

In the beginning, he makes you feel young and vibrant. There is an undeniable physical attraction, and the two of you can't seem to keep your hands off of each other. He is in good shape and has great stamina in the bedroom. Although you can't teach old dog new tricks, cubs are eager and willing to learn. It's refreshing to have someone appreciate the value of your life experiences and not be threatened by your accomplishments. Because of his age, you don't have to face decades of his past relationships and other issues. There are no ex-wives or children—it is all about the two of you.

Unlike men your age, he seems to be full of energy and driven by desires, not obligations. Being around a younger man has actually helped you set and reach your personal goals. His ambition, spontaneous behavior, and energy inspire you.

You feel like this man loves you, so you are willing to put up with his short-term employment and weekend parties. His mother is so happy that the two of you are together because he is no longer in her basement. When he is sporting in your car, the tank is always empty, when he returns.

You have invested a small fortune purchasing a wardrobe for your boy toy to sport while the two of you are out on the town. With proper attire, this young man is eye candy sufficient to satisfy any woman's sweet tooth, and he looks absolutely fabulous on your arm at any gathering!

You feel like you are the happiest that you have been for a very long time and have discovered the fountain of youth in this person. Numerous friends and family members have begged you to rethink your cougar-cub relationship. Where were they when you couldn't get a date and spent countless evenings at home bored and alone? Without a second thought, you let these people know that you are a grown woman, have made your bed, and have a great time sleeping in it! His bedroom manner is to pound on your body unmercifully in an attempt to demonstrate for you how much man he is. You brag to your friends about how you have to take a nap to prepare for him before he gets home.

On the weekends, it is mandatory that he goes out with his boys, and his cell phone is always uncharged or dropping calls. He throws tantrums when he is confronted about his mischievous deeds and will rarely if ever admit to any wrongdoing. He has successfully convinced you that you are insecure about being an older woman with a young man and are hallucinating when you confront him about the things that you have seen with your own, 20/20 restored vision (after cataract surgery on both eyes)!

His life has been full of disappointments and failure, and it is everyone's fault but his own. You will never hear him take the responsibility for past or present mistakes. When the two of you first met, he made you feel like a young woman that was loved, but you are now starting to feel like his mother because of the constant need to complain about his childish behavior.

Let's Talk!

If he's in his twenties and you're in your thirties or forties, there's an enormous difference in what phase of life each of you are in. Men in their twenties are still pretty much boys. Boys make friends around the neighborhood and play video games while their mothers are at work. They may say they want to be in a relationship but may be too young to commit. Many young men really haven't been around long enough to know quite what a relationship consists of or even should look like. A relationship for many young men is having someone to go out with and to have sex with. They're not ready to settle down. Every woman wants a man, but every boy needs a toy.

You're thirties are like silver, and your forties and fifties are worth more than gold. Invest this time in your life intelligently. If your younger man is still going to clubs and hanging out indulging excessively in alcohol with the guys, until the bars close every weekend, he may not be open to finding things you both enjoy—besides sex. But even great sex is not enough to sustain a healthy relationship. Many women feel like they have recaptured part of their youth by hanging out with a younger man that has lots of energy and is often open to exploring new things. However, it can be a rude awakening when they discover that although two of them came to the table, only one had something to bring.

◦⟋◦

Conclusion

Once a man reaches his late thirties and forties, he just about knows what being in a long-term, committed relationship is all about. He is now able to identify what he wants because he has some life experiences to draw from. However, If he's never been married, had kids, been in a long-term committed relationship, and/or had responsibilities, this could pose a problem.

A person who has never had to be responsible for anyone but himself will not be able to comprehend your commitment to your obligations. He will ultimately become agitated when you are not able to just drop the ball and run off to whatever he wants to do. This is particularly true if you have children and he never has. If he's never been married or lived with a woman, he really has no knowledge what is expected of him. Although at first glance he may appear selfish, he's not; he's just never had to think about anyone but himself.

When you are forty or over, you should be tired of playing with other people's children. Let his mother finish where she left off or pay you child support. Don't hang around worrying and catering to him until you look like his mother.

A major attraction of cougar relationships is the sexual aspect. Many cougar women think their male counterparts around the same age are boring and say that they are not satisfied with them in the bedroom. According to recent surveys, many cubs also find the self-assurance and sexual confidence of older ladies a huge turn-on.

Although many cougar-cub relationships can be mutually satisfying, it is important for the cougar to find a kid that has his own toys and is willing to let the cougar play with them. Many cougars make the same mistakes in the second stage of life that they made in their first. The rule is very simple—don't grab a pen; it will not help you to write this down; just remember it. If you must sacrifice your dignity and self-respect to be with a person, it is never worth it at any cost! If you must pick him up, don't get let him drag you down by becoming his free ride. Set limits for yourself, and keep things in perspective. If he only wants to see you when there is something in it for him, then what's in it for you? Whatever you do, if you don't want to be his sugar mommy, then don't marry a baby boy! Never marry a child—and keep in mind that there are many older "children" out there. Kids can be fun to play with, but they make appalling husbands.

One of the most essential parts of any relationship is the way the other person makes you feel. If he makes you feel special and loved, then perhaps this relationship is feasible. But if you are ashamed of your relationship with him when you are out in public and often find yourself feeling used, it is never too late to wake up and smell the coffee. Your relationship should be an asset, not a liability

Today I will Release and Let Go of:

10

My Gut-Buster Story!

~

It was a beautiful, sunny summer day. I was a newly divorced young mom of two boys enjoying a much-needed girls' afternoon out strolling the park with a favorite cousin when a guy drove by, observed me, and said, "There she is." He quickly made a U-turn to come back toward me and my cousin. The gentleman said to me, "I must have your number." He was from another country. Normally, I would never have fulfilled such a demand, but it was something about the approach that I thought was different, and I found myself unable to refuse. However, his conversation and something about him made me keep postponing any dates with him.

One morning, I was feeling particularly depressed about my single status and felt like I needed to start allowing people into my life again to avoid the feeling of emptiness that I could no longer deny inside of me. I finally accepted one of this man's many invitations to dinner at his house after several months of talking with him on the phone and yet knowing that he was not the guy for me. He drove over to pick me up, and when I opened the door, the first thing he said was, "What happened to your skin?" I asked what he meant, and he said, "You were so much darker when I first saw you."

My aunt, who was babysitting for me at the time, laughed and said, "Of course she was darker. We are all darker in the summer." For some reason, the gentleman was really disturbed by the change in my complexion. As I kissed my sons good-bye, a sudden feeling of unhappiness suddenly came over me. I wanted to turn around and run back, but how could I do that to this guy again? The date was set up all erroneous right from the start. I was trying to make myself feel good, and I reached out to something external to do that. I knew I was making a big mistake allowing him to fix me dinner in his home.

When we left for his house, it was a cold, rainy, dreary day, which later turned to heavy fog. We were both pretty silent in the car. I wasn't feeling him, and I think it was mutual. Suddenly, we parked in front of a house, and he explained to me that it was the one he had lived in with his ex-wife. Now, keep in mind that I had talked to this man for about six months on the phone, and he would never go into any detail then about what happened to his marriage. Now he had me parked in front of the house that he shared with his ex, almost as if he was still living there. After about ten minutes, we pulled away, and after a short distance, we arrived at his apartment.

While he was preparing the meal, I sat in the dinette area attached to the kitchen. The guy started talking about his marriage to his ex-wife and how beautiful everything had been. He said she was an American woman and that he had flown people in from all over the world to share in their union. By this time, everything inside of me was telling me that I had to get out of this apartment. He looked like he was going into a daze and almost re-experienced what transpired when he caught his wife underhanded with her ex-boyfriend while he was out of the country. He said for many years, he thought of finding a woman who looked like her and killing her. He then turned around, quickly cutting goat's meat with a knife, and said, "My ex-wife looked a lot like you!" That is when I remembered him saying, "There she is," that day when I met him in the park. It all made sense now.

I remember being frantic, looking around the apartment for anything that could be used if a fight for my life was to occur, because I knew that I was going to do whatever it took to see my two little boys again. Something inside of me told me to remain calm and not to show any fear. I excused myself to the restroom and fell down on my knees in front of the porcelain altar, praying to the God of my understanding to please get me out of this mess that I had managed to get myself into.

When I reentered the room, I sniffed. To my surprise, the man became alarmed. He said, "You have a cold. Why didn't you tell me that you were sick? Do you want me to take you home?" I said yes and thanked him. We rode to my house in complete silence, and I never saw the guy again. He never called.

Some people may say that my complexion looking lighter in the winter made me appear different from his ex-wife and probably saved my life that night, but they don't know the God of my understanding!

⌒○

Let's Talk

People can be really deceptive, and a person should have to earn your trust during your first encounters. The only thing that I should have assumed about this peculiar man was that I would assume nothing. I consider myself fairly intelligent, and although I was newly divorced, I was not new to the world or the people in it. However, I failed this very common life test miserably, and I am very grateful that I am here today and humbly tell my story from many years ago in the hope of helping someone else.

∽つ

Conclusion

Learn to trust your intuition, and never disregard something that worries you so much that you perceive it in your gut. When you have a gut sensation, it is your body's natural way of revealing to you that something is not in accordance with what is proper about the current situation. My gut told me that there was something abnormal about the urgency and the way that the foreign gentleman said, "There she is." I still wonder to this very day about why I never asked the man I met at the park that day what meant when he said "There she is!" What he might have said had I asked? What I know now is that I failed to listen to my intuition when it cautioned me over and over that I did not need to go out with this person. I went with him because I woke up on a cloudy, foggy day, feeling depressed and empty on the inside, and attempted to fill myself up with someone that I actually didn't want to be with because I didn't want to go through the motions that I really needed to go through with *myself.*

Because I didn't take time to get to know this person in every season, I looked very different to this man in the winter and dissimilar from the perception that he had of me in his very much tormented thoughts. It is impossible to get to know a person overnight. Although I spent countless hours with this person on the phone, I didn't know him. Don't let social media or letters confuse you. If you have not had the opportunity to spend time with a person in their home, see them interact around other people, meet their family, coworkers, and friends, in my opinion, you don't truly get to know the authentic person. In many cases, you will find that you have only been introduced to an first impression that they are leaving you with, intentionally or unintentionally. It is our human nature to want to show people our finest side. Personally speaking, with no malice in my heart, I have no intention of ever introducing anyone to any of my character defects early on in a association, if I can help it and I consider myself to be very sincere. All people are different, but life has taught me that trust should be earned by a stranger and not simply given to him. He is not Adam, you are not Eve, and this world is no garden of paradise. Thank you for letting me share!

⁓⊃

Today I will Release and Let Go of:

Free Flyer

~

*The National Center for Victims of Crime
has provided the following information for people
who are victims of domestic violence:*

Identify safe areas of the house where there are no weapons and there are ways to escape. If arguments occur, try to move to those areas.

Don't run to where the children are, as your partner may hurt them as well.

If violence is unavoidable, make yourself a small target. Dive into a corner and curl up into a ball with your face protected and arms around each side of your head, fingers entwined.

If possible, have a phone accessible at all times and know what numbers to call for help. Know where the nearest public phone is located. Know the phone number to your local battered women's shelter. If your life is in danger, call the police.

Let trusted friends and neighbors know of your situation, and develop a plan and visual signal for when you need help.

Teach your children how to get help. Instruct them not to get involved in the violence between you and your partner. Plan a code word to signal to them that they should get help or leave the house.

Tell your children that violence is never right, even when someone they love is being violent. Tell them that neither you nor they are at fault or are the cause of the violence, and that when anyone is being violent, it is important to stay safe.

Practice how to get out safely. Practice with your children.

Plan for what you will do if your children tells your partner of your plan or if your partner otherwise finds out about your plan.

Keep weapons like guns and knives locked away and as inaccessible as possible.

Make a habit of backing the car into the driveway and keeping it fueled. Keep the driver's door unlocked and others locked—for a quick escape.

Don't wear scarves or long jewelry that could be used to strangle you.

Create several plausible reasons for leaving the house at different times of the day or night.

Leaving a Relationship

Preparing to Leave
When You Leave
After You Leave
Because violence could escalate when someone tries to leave, here are some things to keep in mind before you leave:

Keep any evidence of physical abuse, such as pictures of injuries.

Keep a journal of all violent incidences, noting dates, events, and threats made, if possible. Keep your journal in a safe place.

Know where you can go to get help. Tell someone what is happening to you.

If you are injured, go to a doctor or an emergency room and report what happened to you. Ask that they document your visit.

Plan with your children and identify a safe place for them, like a room with a lock or a friend's house where they can go for help. Reassure them that their job is to stay safe, not to protect you.

Contact your local shelter and find out about laws and other resources available to you before you have to use them during a crisis. WomensLaw.org has state-by-state legal information.

Acquire job skills or take courses at a community college as you can.

Try to set money aside or ask friends or family members to hold money for you.

(Some of this information is adapted from: Copyright © 1998 by the National Center for Victims of Crime. This information may be freely distributed, provided that it is distributed free of charge, in its entirety and includes this copyright notice.)

Legal Info
There are some legal actions you can take to help keep yourself safe from your abusive partner. The hotline does not give legal advice, nor are we legal advocates, but there are some great resources available to you in your community.

Please call 1-800-799-SAFE (7233) or chat with us and our advocates can connect you with resources for legal help.

You can also visit WomensLaw.org and search state by state for information on laws including restraining orders and child custody information.

Protective Orders and Restraining Orders

A protective order can help protect you immediately by legally keeping your partner from physically coming near you, harming you, or harassing you, your children, or your family members.

This legal documentation to keep your abusive partner away from you can often contain provisions related to custody, finance, and more.

While protective orders may be able to put a stop to physical abuse, psychological abuse is still possible—so a protective order should never replace a safety plan.

If you already have a protective order, it should be kept on you at all times, and copies should be given to your children and anyone they might be with—especially when you're leaving your partner.

You can get an application for a protective order at:
- Courthouses
- Women's shelters
- Volunteer legal services offices
- Some police stations

Other Legal Actions

You also have the right to file a charge against your partner for things such as criminal assault, aggravated assault, harassment, stalking, or interfering with child custody. Ask a volunteer legal services organization (attorneys who provide free legal services to low-income individuals) or an advocacy group in your area about the policies in your local court.

Not a US citizen? Learn more at Casa de Esperanza about your rights as an immigrant and read more on our site.

According to the Violence Against Women Act (VAWA), immigrant women who are experiencing domestic violence and are married to abusers who are US citizens or legal permanent residents may qualify to self-petition for legal status under VAWA.

About Tamara Neal

~

Tamara Neal is a certified domestic relationship coach, domestic violence advocate, and the owner and founder of a full-service residential adult assisted living center.

Neal learned to trust her instincts while employed as an emergency communication technician for the Baltimore County 911 Center. For years she listened to screams and terror as callers bore the brunt of toxic relationships. In the seeming eternity between calling 911 and the arrival of the police, Neal was the only help available for the person on the other end of the phone. During this time she received a national diploma in emergency dispatch.

Her dispatch experience gave Neal the authority needed to write The World's Top Ten Worst Men for Women Guide, Relationship Bloopers & Blunders, two children's books Kinship and Friendship.

Neal currently lives in Maryland with her husband. Together they have four sons, a daughter, and numerous grandchildren.

Contact Author Tamara Neal
(888) 503-1575
www.tamaraneal.com
www.venomousrelationships.com

Also Available from
Tamara's Books By
Tamara Neal

Available wherever books are sold

THE WORLD'S TOP TEN WORST MEN FOR
WOMEN GUIDE
By Tamara R. Neal
"An affirming guide to dangerous relationships that skips
the jargon in favor of a personal, direct message."

KIRKUS REVIEW

A heartfelt, personal look at the various abusive relationships women can find themselves in.

Neal intends to prevent other women from facing the sort of relationship heartbreak she has not only seen in many friends and acquaintances, but also experienced herself. The result is a Top 10 list of male types to avoid. While the guide is addressed to heterosexual women, the 10 types will be bad news in any relationship. Each of the ten chapters focuses on a different painful or dangerous situation, but as Neal notes, any one person can possess any combination of the traits. The book calls out obvious red-flag behaviors such as addiction, abuse and adultery, but it also highlights lesser-known signs of relationship trouble, including indications that a potential partner is only interested in a one-night stand or that a partner hasn't gotten over his previous relationship and is thus in no position to make the new one work. Throughout the book, Neal reminds the reader that there's only one person she can and should change: herself. The energy a woman spends chasing one of these bad-news partners is energy that, Neal says, could be spent learning to improve and care for herself, which would help in building the internal strength needed to avoid any partner who doesn't trust or care for her. Unlike some guides to abusive relationships, Neal's book skips the traditional language of psychology; there's no discussion of the "cycle of abuse" or a 12-step recovery. Rather, Neal takes a personal approach, encouraging women to recognize and reclaim what they might already know: They'll only find the self-confidence they seek within themselves. Since the style is so personal, the text can at times be difficult to follow; it reads like a coffee chat with close friends, with sudden shifts in topic or tactic that can cause a moment's confusion. Nevertheless, the message is clear: You're worth more than the 10 types of people on this list, if you let yourself be.

An affirming guide to dangerous relationships that skips the jargon in favor of a personal, direct message.

KIRKUS REVIEW

Neal's (Kinship, 2013, etc.) latest picture book presents an idealized view of universal friendship.

Neal's first children's book references the I Have a Dream Elementary School and conveys an understanding of Martin Luther King Jr.'s hope, expressed in his speech of that name, that the time would come in America when people of all backgrounds would be joined "in a beautiful symphony of brotherhood." Neal expresses this vision through the narration of Christopher, a dog and "friend to all of mankind," who invites readers to consider various types of friendship. Beginning with real and imaginary friends, he then covers diversity of hair and sleeping arrangements before moving on to body type, likes and dislikes, disabilities and animal friends. No matter the differences, Christopher says, all his friends "are friendly, in their own special way!" Also touched upon are friends who speak different languages or live in different types of housing; friends who use wheelchairs or are deaf, sick or blind; and those who live in a home with two parents of the same gender. The diversity of these friends' ethnic backgrounds is further revealed in colorful digital illustrations. Christopher concludes with claims that friends are never bullies, and they should always be friendly and estimable. The final lines demonstrate the book's overly optimistic view of reality: "It takes all types of friendships to / make the world go around. / Friends are really special people, / that are very easily found!" The fact that the narrator is a dog doesn't seem to matter much; there's no story, and very few of the images actually contain a dog. Similarly, despite the book's summery tone, it offers no guidance for finding friends or tackling the challenges of friendship.

A light and breezy view of an inclusive, perfect world in which everyone can be friends.

Kinship

Relationship book for kids

Tamara Neal

Overview

Kinship discusses the changes that occur in families as children are born and children grow. Its objective is to teach that individuals and families are alike and different, but at the core, we are all the same. The author addresses the differing abilities that we each have and will encounter-whether as children or adults.

Sleeping With the Enemy

When the bar closes and the smoke clears, it becomes noticeably apparent you have wrote yourself a check, despite having insufficient funds to cash it! Now in a state of complete psychological bankruptcy, you find yourself in a committed relationship with a woman that apparently was only a good catch because no one else was fishing! After disregarding several legitimate informants, declining to believe the obvious, existing in a constant state of denial, you must now man-up and sadly contemplate what has become irrefutable. The woman that you gave your heart to is a seductress that had sat and waited for a prey.

It was early in the morning, in the middle of the night, when the lips of this alluring woman sounded so sweet; her soft words were captivating and hypnotic. She owned the room with an outer beauty that was glamorous, to say the least. The words that came out of her mouth were enough to have almost any man stumbling to the slaughter, on the right night!

One year, two babies later, you have come to the realization that the first date never ended. How did things go from having an out of control fantasy coming true, with great sex, lies, wild private parties, to married with children? Things began to move so fast, it seemed without notice one day she left a tooth brush and a curling iron in your bathroom and the next day a moving truck was at your front door.

The following seasons of the liaison appeared to be totally different from the sizzling summer that you met. Shortly after she moved in things about her personality that were not revealed before are now beginning to fall into place. Winter, is brutal and filled with continuous brisk cold episodes of her ranting and raving endlessly about absolutely nothing understandable. Just when you think that you have had, about as much as you can take and the end is inevitable, she announces that she is pregnant. Suddenly you feel the cool sensation of someone attempting to tie a ball and chain to one of your ankles. It has now dawned on you that the storm has just started and phase three is now in effect!

Some days you can actually see the light at the end of the tunnel before it turns out to be another oncoming train. Needless to say, even the good days are nothing to write home to mom about. As you glance back over your relationship with this individual, vision of what use to be pleasurable now seem faint. Everything that you do is wrong or never good enough for her. Your life is now only lived on life's terms when she is in agreement or the author of them. Reality and her world are two different things and no one is going to tell her otherwise.

Trust is basically nonexistent in the mind of this very self-absorbed woman who has managed to infiltrate your world. Without cause, her days are spent rummaging through your things, as if she has a warrant and is in the process of a raid. She allocates countless hours investigating and interrogating anyone that has been in your company, looking for grounds to base her next argument. Her nights consist of racing thoughts about the things that she thinks she found during the day. Your cell phone has become a stalking device that can and will be used against you at her convenience. Your cell phone also known as her tracking device must be answered at all times, in an effort to avoid an unnecessary interrogation later. Under her law you are guilty, simply because she said you are! Only because you have been brought up to believe that if you faint in the day of adversity that your strength is small, you continue to weather the storm and it is not inconspicuous by any means.

One day you arrive home to what appears to be another one of her illicit examinations of your personal possessions and without notice you are suddenly being attacked by a woman that is very irate. Although your upbringing will not permit you to counter attack, you are human and have now been placed in harm's way. Your attempts to restrain her have only made matters worse because in her mind you are now acting aggressive and argumentative. Eventually she becomes so hostile and out of control that you decide to leave, however she shadows you, in her vehicle. Resembling something off of and action movie, she begins ramming her car into your car, in an unwavering effort to run you in your vehicle, off the road. The state of affairs is out of control and you can only envision that it is going to take an outside source to stop it! Suddenly, you see police cars coming from every direction and she is arrested on numerous charges. There are several eye witnesses that saw the incident and called the police. One of the officers asked you, if you were okay and if you would like to go to the hospital. It has suddenly dawned on you that you are a victim of a violent domestic, however you can't or don't want to believe it. The next day you attempt to drop the charges only to find that they were so serious that the charges could not be dropped because the state picked them up. So you bail her out of jail and for some reason you feel empathy for her. She promises that it will never happen again and begins to act like the woman that you always wanted. She apologized and explains to you how you made her do it, when she found pictures of your old girlfriends, in your belongings. With tears in her eyes she acknowledged that she has severe trust issues, as a direct result of being deceived by every man that ever promised to love her exclusively, in all of her prior relationships.

You go to work exhausted and ashamed after what has been a totally humiliating weekend. Several coworkers immediately inquire about the apparently vandalized condition of your car, so you make up a lie. Your cell phone is smashed however you are still able to use it and this does not go without being noticed by several suspicious looking co-workers, as well. You find yourself covering up your abusive relationship by saying unbelievable things, like the cat attacked you. When you leave work she is sitting outside on the parking lot and asked "why you haven't been answering you're obviously, severely damaged, tracking device?" Before you could answer, she asked "who was that woman that I saw you speaking with as I drove up?" One of your worst fears has come true; she is going to act out on your job!

Let's Talk!

Men are essentially inaudible on the issue when they find themselves in an abusive relationship because of the perception that men are physically stronger and should be able to subdue a female attacker easily. Those men who do report physical violence are more likely to be ridiculed–both by law enforcement and by the public–than women are. Many men suffer in abusive relationships unannounced to them because they think that abuse is only physical; however there are many forms of abuse such as, emotional, economic, or psychological actions or threats of actions that influence another person. This includes any behaviors that intimidate, manipulate, humiliate, isolate, frighten, terrorize, threaten, blame, hurt, injure, or wound someone just to name a few.

Conclusion

The following examples are forms of abuse that many men silently fall victim to on the daily bases:

1. When a man is constantly being threatened that he will never see his children again if he does not comply with what the woman wants, this is abuse.
2. Constantly being humiliated in private or public.
3. Any person that has been forced to stay away from people that they love against their will, without cause, is being controlled and this too is abuse.
4. When a man undergoes any form of a physical attack such as being kicked, punched, scratched, choked, spit on, slapped or having things thrown at him, he is unquestionably a victim of domestic violence.
5. When a man finds himself trying to keep peace by not showing his children from a previous relationship consideration because of fear that it will cause his mate to become hostile, this is abuse.
6. If a man is constantly being threaten with being taken to child support and taken for everything that he has if he is not compliant, this is a form of control and therefore also abuse.
7. Whenever a man's personal property and belonging are intentionally destroyed as a form of punishment for whatever reason this is abuse.
8. When a man is called names like dumb, stupid, fat, ugly, loser, old, crazy, useless, and host of other French words on the regular bases by his mate, this is abuse.
9. When a man is constantly being put down and degraded in front of his children this is also abuse.
10. Being intentionally ignored and isolated unprovoked, for long periods of time is abuse.

Okay where do we go from here? Hopefully not back to this woman. This relationship is definitely not reconcilable without some form of formal intervention. This woman appears to be sick and you are now suffering from the wreckage of her past. Some of the trauma could have been avoided if you allowed yourself to get to know her first from the inside out opposed to the outside in. The only way to accomplish this would be for you to get to know her in every season. Most people have their best foot forward when they first meet a person. However, if you hang around long enough you will get to know the real person as they introduce their self while dealing with life on life's terms. Emotion such as fear, anger, sadness, disappointment and disgust will teach you everything that you need to know!

CPSIA information can be obtained
at www.ICGtesting.com
Printed in the USA
FFOW05n2031061215